GEORGIA, ARMENIA, AND AZERBAIJAN

By
Elizabeth Roberts

The Millbrook Press
Brookfield, Connecticut

©Aladdin Books Ltd 1992

Designed and produced by
Aladdin Books Ltd
28 Percy Street
London W1P 9FF

First published in the
United States in 1992 by
The Millbrook Press
2 Old New Milford Road
Brookfield, Connecticut 06804

The consultant is Dr. John Channon of the School of
Slavonic and Eastern European Studies, London, UK.

Series Design:David West
Designer:Rob Hillier
Editor:Claire Watts
Picture Research:Emma Krikler

Library of Congress Cataloging-in-Publication Data

Roberts, Elizabeth. 1944-
    Georgia, Armenia, and Azerbaijan/by Elizabeth
Roberts: John Channon, consultant.
        p. cm – (Former Soviet States)
    Includes bibliographical references and index.
    Summary: Discusses the political instability in the
Caucasian states of Georgia, Armenia, and Azerbaijan
    ISBN 1-56294-309-X (lib. bdg.) :
    1. Soviet Union, Southern--Juvenile literature.
2. Azerbaijan--Juvenile literature. 3. Georgian S.S.R.–
Juvenile literature. 4. Armenian S.S.R.–Juvenile literature.
(1. Georgian S.S.R. 2. Armenian S.S.R. 3. Azerbaijan.)
I. Title. II. Series.
DK509.R57 1992
947'.9--dc20   92-2242 CIP AC

Printed in Belgium   All rights reserved

CONTENTS

INTRODUCTION

Armenia, Georgia, and Azerbaijan were three of the fifteen members of the former Union of Soviet Socialist Republics (U.S.S.R.). Together they are sometimes called Transcaucasia, or the Caucasus. They occupy one of the world's great crossroads. This is where Europe meets Asia. Over the centuries, Christian and Muslim empires have clashed in the area, leaving a rich, sometimes explosive, cultural and ethnic legacy. More languages are spoken here than in any area of comparable size in the world.

To the west of Transcaucasia is the beautiful Black Sea, leading to the trading routes of the Mediterranean beyond the Bosporus. To the east is the Caspian Sea and the ancient Silk Road to China. North, beyond the high, steep Caucasus Mountains, which give the region its name, lies the vast, powerful expanse of Russia. To the south are Transcaucasia's two other most powerful neighbors, Turkey and Iran.

4

Arctic Ocean

Zemlya Frantsa Josifa

70° E

80° E

90° E

Severnaya Zemlya

120° E

130° E

140° E

150° E

160° E

170° E

Novo Sibirskiye Ostrova

Laptev Sea

Kara Sea

Kolyma

Bering Sea

Lena

Yenisey

Sea of Okhotsk

50° N

RUSSIAN FEDERATION

Sakhalin

JAPAN

Trans-Siberian Railroad

Lake Baikal

Vladivostok

40° N

MONGOLIA

NORTH KOREA

SOUTH KOREA

CHINA

0	250	500	750	1000	1250 MILES

0	500	1000	1500	2000 KILOMETERS

THE STATES TODAY

Marchers demonstrate peacefully for an end to the communist system.

The Soviet Union came to an end in December 1991, and with it the last of the great European empires. Now Georgia, Armenia, and Azerbaijan are independent states. Their citizens have elected governments from local candidates, and they are no longer ruled by officials appointed by the Communist Party in Moscow.

Armenia and Azerbaijan decided to be founding members of the Commonwealth of Independent States (C.I.S.), a federation formed after the breakup of the Soviet Union to enable an orderly disposal of assets to take place. This meant trying to agree, for instance, on what was to become of the massive stocks of weapons and troops of the former Soviet army scattered around these countries, as well as what new terms were to be agreed for trade between the new countries.

Independence

On September 21, 1991, the people of Armenia voted for independence, and they did so by a majority of 99 percent. Armenia was declared a sovereign state outside the Soviet Union by a vote of 213 to 0. In October 1991, the people of Armenia elected Levon Ter-Petrosyan president, with an 82.3 percent majority, from a strong field of five candidates.

Troubled transition

Georgia has experienced a more troubled transition to independence. Elections in May 1991 brought to power Zviad Gamsakhurdiya by a massive 87 percent majority. Five months later, Gamsakhurdiya was driven into exile, after bitter street battles in the Georgian capital, Tbilisi, and other cities left hundreds dead and many buildings destroyed. Gamsakhurdiya's political opponents had accused him of undemocratic measures against them, and of failure to institute promised market reforms. Gamsakhurdiya was also criticized for his decision not to opt for membership in the C.I.S., and for his reaction to the news in the attempted August coup in Moscow, when he had apparently ordered Georgian troops to lay down their arms. Sporadic fighting continued in other parts of Georgia, such as in the formerly autonomous region known as South Ossetia, due to the demands of inhabitants to be reunited with their fellow Ossetians across the border in Russia.

Eduard Shevardnadze was appointed acting head of state in Georgia, in March 1992. Shevardnadze was a former foreign minister of the Soviet Union and before that he was the communist leader of Georgia.

Eduard Schevardnadze

Bloodshed in Baku

Azerbaijan also suffered bloodshed on the streets of the capital, Baku, before Soviet troops finally received orders not to obstruct the nationalist independence movement any longer. Moscow-backed

Ayaz Mutalibov was succeeded in March 1992 by Yagub Mamdov, following massive street protests at the failure of Azeri troops to protect the Azeri minority living in the disputed area of Nagorno-Karabakh from attacks by Armenian nationalists who want the area to become part of Armenia (see page 21).

Calls for independence

The movement toward independence came both from the people of the former Soviet Union and from politicians.

Zviad Gamsakhurdiya speaks in Georgia's parliament.

Azeri boys wave a homemade Azeri flag.

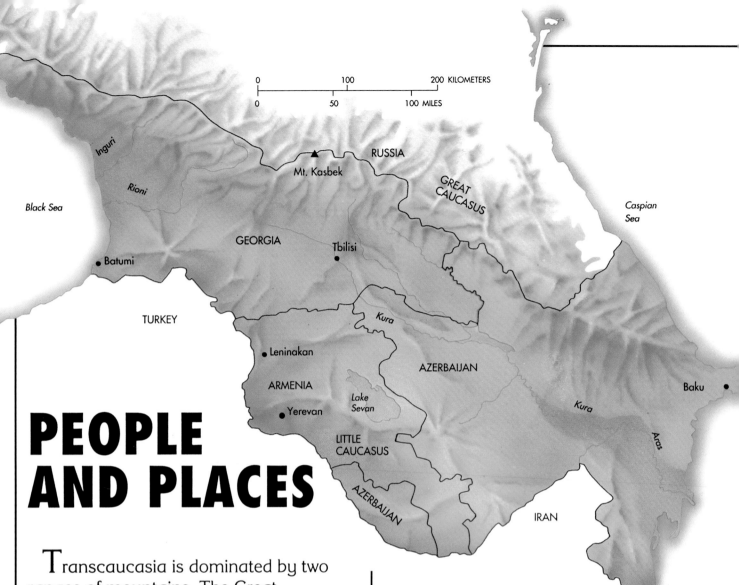

PEOPLE AND PLACES

Transcaucasia is dominated by two ranges of mountains. The Great Caucasus stretches across 621 miles (1,000 kilometers) to the north, and the Little Caucasus cuts the region off from Turkey, to the south. The mountains rise to 16,500 feet (5,000 meters), making travel by land difficult. The Black Sea encloses the region to the west, and the Caspian Sea to the east. The region is situated on a fault in the earth's crust, making it subject to earthquakes.

A varied climate

The climate in the region ranges from eternal snow on some of the mountain peaks of the Caucasus, to Mediterranean mildness on the Black Sea Riviera, through subtropical zones and the dry desert plain of the Kura River in southeast Azerbaijan.

An Armenian woman sits in the rubble of her home after the 1988 earthquake.

Religion and language

Against a background of seventy years of determinedly secular government, which sometimes actively persecuted organized religion, Armenia and Georgia are among the oldest Christian states in the world. They both adopted Christianity as a state religion in the third century A.D. In fact, Armenia is one of the oldest centers of civilization in the world.

Due to repeated foreign invasions throughout its history, up to eighty-three languages are spoken in the region, some by just a single village. Armenian is an ancient branch of Indo-European. Georgian is not Indo-European, and is not related to Russian in any way. The curious Georgian alphabet was probably developed from eastern Aramaic.

The people of Azerbaijan, on the other hand, are mainly Muslim, sharing their language, traditions, and ethnic origins with their Turkish neighbors, to whom they still look today for international support.

Armenian Orthodox priest in ceremonial robes

The Armenian earthquake

On December 7, 1988, a massive earthquake destroyed three major cities and 150 villages in northern Armenia. Nearly 25,000 died in and around Leninakan, Spitak, and Stephanavan, and half a million were left homeless. Many millions of dollars of international aid were collected to help rebuild the homes, hospitals, schools, and factories. Progress has been hampered by the political unrest in the region.

Mount Elbrus, in the Caucasus

A VITAL ROUTE

From the earliest times, the region covered by Georgia, Armenia, and Azerbaijan has been seen as a vital link between east and west, conquered and reconquered by opposing powers. The first of the many tribal invasions, which were to become a pattern repeated throughout the history of the region, began toward the end of the third millenium B.C. The native early Bronze Age culture of the area was shaken by an influx of Indo-European people from the northern Caucasus and the Eurasian steppes. The next arrivals were invaders from Turkey who had been driven into the Caucasus by people from the Aegean and Mediterranean between 1900 and 1200 B.C.

Greeks and Romans

The next major external influence on the culture and political history of the region was the establishment of a vast empire, from 334-323 B.C. by Alexander the Great, a Greek from Macedonia. He died in 323 B.C. leaving his generals in charge of his conquered lands, including parts of Armenia and Georgia, which paid dues to the heir of Alexander in the Greek-ruled city of Antioch in Turkey.

Tigranes the Great

For a time, Armenia was a rich and powerful state under King Tigranes the Great (95-55 B.C.). He ruled over a vast territory between the Black, Caspian, and Mediterranean seas. His capital was Tigrankert in northern Mesopotamia. Then came the Roman armies of Pompey in 66 B.C., which took Tigrankert and marched as far as the Kura River. Other great powers influenced the area too: the Seleucids, the Persians, the Parthians, the Medes, and the Scythians based in the Near and Middle East.

Treasures have been found in the area, left by invaders.

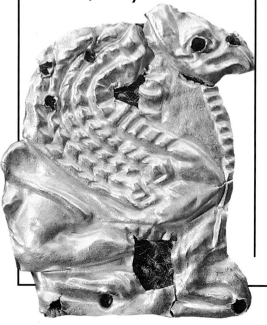

A Greek statue found just over the border in Turkey

Myths and legends of the Caucasus

The legend of King Midas, cursed in Greek legend to turn everything he touched to gold, may be based on the Meskhian King Mita (seventh century B.C.), who ruled southern Georgia.

Jason and the Argonauts are thought to have sailed up the Black Sea coast from their base in the Aegean, to western Georgia in search of the Golden Fleece. Fleece is used to trap gold in the local rivers.

Noah's Ark was supposed to have settled on Mount Ararat, once within the borders of Armenia. Legend has it that Armenians are descended from Noah's great-great-grandson, Haik. Armenians call Armenia Hayakstan, or the Land of Haik.

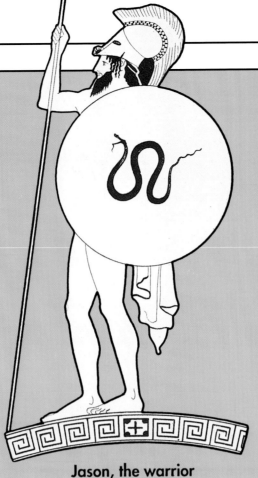

Jason, the warrior

The animals enter the ark.

THE RELIGIOUS SPLIT

Armenia became the first state in the world to adopt Christianity, in A.D. 301. Georgia adopted Christianity as its official state religion under King Mirian III in A.D. 330. In Azerbaijan, there was an early tradition of fire worship, known as Zoroastrianism. Later, the majority of Azeris were converted to Islam.

The Muslim threat

In A.D. 642, the Arabs conquered Azerbaijan. Throughout the region's history, Christian Georgia and Armenia have been under threat from the Muslim communities which surround them. For the three hundred years after adopting Christianity, Georgia was torn by the conflict between the Christian Byzantine Empire and the Islamic Persian Empire. The Arabs finally took Tbilisi in A.D. 645 and installed an emir there, but allowed eastern Georgia to be ruled by Georgian princes under Arab control.

A richly decorated icon

In Armenia in 885, the Arabs set Ashot the Great up as king. His dynasty, the Bagratids, flourished because they were diplomatic in their dealings with their Arab overlords. Ashot III (952-977) transferred the Bagratid capital to the city of Ani, which was to become one of the most beautiful medieval cities, and a center for art and literature. The Bagratids ruled over a century and a half of exceptional prosperity until they were conquered, first by the Christian Byzantine army (1045) and then by the Seljuk Turks (1064).

This Armenian temple is about fifteen hundred years old.

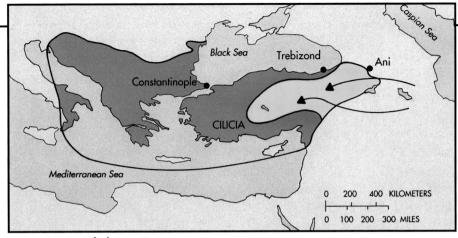

Byzantine & Seljuk invasions

- ▓ Extent of Byzantine Empire until 1064
- ░ Area ceded to Seljuks in 1064
- → Movement of Armenians

Cilicia

In 1080, Armenians fleeing from Turkish rule in their own country founded the kingdom of Cilicia on the northeastern corner of the Mediterranean Sea. The kingdom was ruled by a relative of the Bagratid rulers of Armenia. Cilicia finally fell to the sultan of Egypt in 1375.

The Seljuk Turks had been converted to the Sunni sect of Islam in 960. They were a confederation of tribes ruled over by the "ulema," the teachers and religious leaders of Islam. The Seljuks demanded tribute from the peoples that they overran, rather than taking over administratively.

Sunnis and Shi'ites

Muslims throughout the world have been divided for over 1,000 years. Sunnis believe that the leader of Islam should be elected. Shi'ites believe that the descendants of the family of Muhammad, founder of Islam, have a right to rule. Today 70 percent of Azeri Muslims are Shi'ite, and 30 percent are Sunnis.

Islamic scholars in Azerbaijan

من نقتربوا اليه باعتاق الاسارى واطلاق... فاستشعر المتصرف من... القول... ولم يبق نور... من بنهم ومعه سبعة يده فارس

من جنوده ونفاوة اصحابه... فلما وصل الى ساحل... وجد جامدا... فامر بان يوضع التبن على الجليد ووضع عليه... فلما وصل اليهم العسكر

العذر كان قد اسا... النهار وطلعت الثمر... ودل المتصرف على خط امل... كتابا بعث فيه عليكم ماتركم فيه من امواج الكربة وما

فاسا... من شدايد الغزو... وبلجا... الى كنف اشفاقه وظفر... ايسا لدوسلم نعام انقياده الى بـ مراده وقال... شمق...

Mongol archers cross a frozen river, about 1300.

THE MIDDLE AGES

Under David the Builder (1089-1124) and his granddaughter Queen Tamara (1184-1212), Georgia enjoyed a golden age of territorial expansion while the Turks were under pressure from the first Crusade. David took power in Tbilisi in 1122, and it became a center of religious tolerence. David was known as "Aghmashenebeli," or the builder, because he encouraged the development and construction of magnificent buildings such as monasteries and churches. During Tamara's reign, Georgia reached its largest extent, stretching over the whole Caucasus region.

Invading hordes

Attacks on the Caucasus came not just from the region's Muslim neighbors. Cities in Azerbaijan were attacked and plundered by the Viking warriors from Scandinavia (known locally as Varangians) on several occasions between 750 and 943. The Vikings did not settle in the area, but raided it from settlements further north.

Mongol invasion

But worse was to come. The Mongol invasion hit the whole region in 1220. The Mongols were a savage horde of nomadic horsemen led by Genghis Khan. They had conquered China before turning to sweep across the Caucasus and the southern Russian plains, taking every city and leaving a pyramid of human skulls behind them. The first Mongols were neither Christian nor

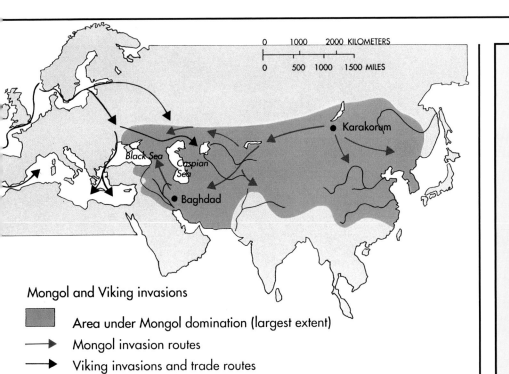

Mongol and Viking invasions

Area under Mongol domination (largest extent)

→ Mongol invasion routes

→ Viking invasions and trade routes

Muslim. Their method of administration was to collect heavy tribute from their conquered subjects, including taxes on east-west trade. But there were positive aspects to Mongol domination, too. Mongol protection improved the security of trade routes, and the Mongols introduced the first paper money to the West. During the period of Mongol domination, Azerbaijan was ruled by Mongol leaders known as khans.

A mosque influenced by Mongol architecture

Viking artifacts

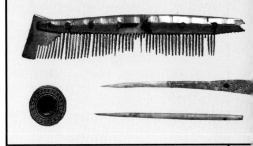

The Knight in the Tiger Skin

The epic twelfth century poem by Shota Rustaveli occupies a central place in Georgian culture similar to that of Shakespeare in the English language. It is said that, at one time, a Georgian woman could not marry until she could recite the whole poem by heart. The poem is a long epic tale of knightly love. Its author is said to have been born in the Georgian village of Rustavi, educated in Athens, and returned to Georgia to work as a private secretary to Queen Tamara. He later became a monk, some say because he had fallen hopelessly in love with his royal employer. His poem ends with a warning of the troubled times ahead for Georgia:

"Their deeds are ended, like a dream at night

With them, their golden age has ended too."

TURKISH PRESSURE

In 1453, Constantinople, for a thousand years the capital of the Christian Byzantine Empire, fell to the Ottoman Turks. This momentous event in world history left the Christian kingdoms of Georgia and Armenia cut off from western Christendom and signaled the onset of a period of intense Islamic pressure. It also disrupted the traditional east-west trading routes and led directly to Columbus' attempt to discover a western route to India in 1492.

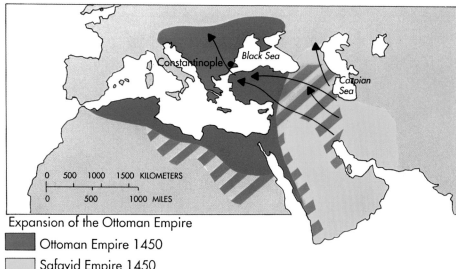

Expansion of the Ottoman Empire

█ Ottoman Empire 1450

░ Safavid Empire 1450

▨ Ottoman expansion by 1566

→ East-west trade routes

The Ottoman Empire

The Ottoman Empire was huge and powerful. When an area came under Ottoman control, they would capture local people, forcibly convert them to Islam, and use them for military service.

The Ottoman armies pushed north and west, up the Black Sea coast, taking the last forlorn outpost of the Byzantine Empire at Trebizond in 1461; they crossed the Bosporos to Bulgaria, Serbia, Boznia, Herzogovina and down to Albania. They besieged Vienna in Austria and Vicenza in Italy, took Cracow in Poland, and defeated the King of Hungary at Mohacs in 1526.

Divided Georgia

A rival dynasty arose in Persia, the Shi'ite Safavids, who captured Tbilisi in 1548. The Peace of Amasia in 1555 divided the area into two spheres of influence: Ottoman in the west, and Safavid in the east. For the next 250 years, the kings of Kartli (central Georgia) ruled by permission of the shahs of Persia, and the whole of the Caucasus came under Turkish domination.

Ivan the Terrible, the Russian Tsar, became interested in the position of the little Christian kingdoms on his southern border, but he was

A Constantinople church

The Ottoman Topkapi palace

View of Constantinople

powerless to act against the mighty Islamic forces. It was to take two centuries before the roles were reversed.

Armenian traders

In the fourteenth and fifteenth centuries, there were Armenian trading communities throughout the world, as far apart as Paris, Venice, Astrakhan, and Calcutta. Armenians dominated Caucasian trade, dealing in wine, leather, carpets, jam, and cheese. Today Armenian communities can be found all over the world.

The Cossacks

The Cossacks were warriors who settled along the banks of the Don and Dnepr rivers in the fourteenth century. They were members of the Eastern Orthodox Church who had fled from the rule of Polish-Lithuanian overlords in southern Russia who were trying to enforce the supremacy of the Roman Catholic Church.

The Cossacks were outlaws seeking freedom from serfdom. They fought on behalf of the Russian tsars defending the southern borders of Russia. The word "cossack" comes from the Turkish "kasakh," meaning outlaw or adventurer.

Suleiman, head of the Ottoman Empire, 1520-66

TSARIST RULE

Russia's foreign policy was aimed at securing its expanding empire's southern flank and developing trade routes. In 1772, Peter the Great sent a military expedition which captured the Caspian port of Derbend. In 1801, the Christian king of central Georgia, Georgi XII, decided to sign his authority over to Tsar Paul I, in exchange for Russian protection. Then Baku and the Khanate of Kuba in modern Azerbaijan were annexed by Russian troops. Treaties were signed in 1812 and 1813 with the Turks and Persians. All their claims to Georgia, Abkhazia, and Daghestan were ceded to Russia. After the battle of Ezerum in 1828, Turkey and Russia reached an uneasy agreement that was not to be fundamentally shaken until the beginning of World War I.

Stability
By the end of the nineteenth century, the three republics of the Transcaucasus had

In 1915, the Turkish government suddenly moved against the Armenian population, killing more than a million people.

settled down under a Russian governor general based in Tbilisi. All major decisions affecting the region were made in St. Petersburg, the capital of Tsarist Russia, a thousand miles to the north. Important local officials such as the justices of the peace were also Russian.

With the stability of Russian protection, the economy had a chance to develop. The region's wealth depended on the export or transshipment of raw materials, such as manganese ore, lumber, dried raisins, palm wood, walnut wood, walnuts, tobacco, silk, wool, fruits, and raw and manufactured hides. Grain and petroleum were exported from Baku, Poti, and Batumi. Millions of gallons of wine were produced annually, some of it exported to France where it was relabeled "Burgundy" and sold as expensive French wine! Russian rule brought railroads, and the Georgian Military Highway running north-south across the great divide of the Caucasus mountains, making Georgia, Armenia, and Azerbaijan more accessible than ever before.

World War I

But the fate of the Caucasus was to be determined by political events far away that precipitated World War I. The war drew Turkey and Russia in on opposing sides. Turkey was on the side of the Central Powers led by Germany, while Russia joined the Allies with Britain and France. The human and economic toll of year after year of trench warfare was terrible. Great armies advanced only yards from fixed positions at the cost of thousands of lives.

Crisis in Russia

At last, the simmering political crisis in Russia was brought to a head. From early in the nineteenth century, there had been dissatisfaction in Russia. No one in the country was free except the tsar. At the very bottom were serfs who were little better than slaves. Crippling taxes were levied to pay for the army and the whole political system was corrupt. Although some reforms were made during the century, notably the emancipation of the serfs in 1861, they made little difference to people's lives. A revolution in 1905 was overthrown. The horrors of World War I were the final straw. In 1917, the Tsar abdicated and the February Revolution followed. In October, a small group of Bolsheviks led by their founder, Vladimir Ilyich Lenin, seized power in the capital of Russia, St. Petersburg (renamed Petrograd during World War I). Civil war broke out.

Tsar Nicholas II

Russian soldiers in the trenches during World War I

REVOLUTION!

After the coup of 1917 in Russia, the three countries of the Caucasus enjoyed a brief period of independence. There were democratically elected governments in Baku, Yerevan, and Tbilisi. But these were to be short-lived.

The Red Army moves in
Baku fell to the Soviet Red Army in April 1920. Using Azerbaijan as their base, the Red Army drove the Social Democratic government from Tbilisi, forcing the leaders to flee west to Batumi, then into exile abroad.

Armenia surrendered to the Red Army in preference to the threat of being overrun by Turkey. The hard-pressed new Soviet government in Moscow, led by Lenin, was anxious to establish firm borders as soon as possible. They hastily made peace with Turkey on humiliating terms, ceding disputed Armenian territory to Turkey.

Between 1922 and 1936, Armenia, Georgia, and Azerbaijan were ruled from Moscow as a single Transcaucasian republic. In 1936, they each became constituent members of the Union of Soviet Socialist Republics, with theoretical rights of secession.

Stalin
Despite the fact that Joseph Stalin, ruler of the Soviet Union after Lenin's death in 1924, was a Georgian, Stalinist repressions in the whole area were just as harsh as elsewhere in the Soviet Union. An attempted uprising in Georgia was brutally quashed, and more than 5,000 people were executed. Between 1936 and 1937, many writers, scientists, and other intellectuals were shot or transported to labor camps.

As in other parts of the Soviet Empire, the Stalin era in the Caucasus was marked by a ruthless drive to set up state-owned and centrally controlled heavy industry and agriculture, along with the repression of all human rights. Stalin accused some of the tribes of the Caucasus, such as the Meskhetian Turks, of having collaborated with the Nazi invaders. To punish them, Stalin organized widespread deportations to distant areas of Central Asia, wiping their autonomous republic homelands from the map: an unwelcome legacy of bitterness for the future.

A prison camp, or gulag, in Siberia

Nagorno-Karabakh

The problem over Nagorno-Karabakh began during the revolution. Nagorno-Karabakh's population is mainly Armenian, and the territory was part of Armenia until the eleventh century, when it was conquered by the Turks. Following the October Revolution of 1917, Armenia and Azerbaijan disputed territorial rights over Nagorno-Karabakh. When the communists seized power in Baku, Armenia had to decide between acceding to Soviet power or being overrun by Turkey. The new communist government offered to give Karabakh to Armenia, if Armenia joined the Soviet Union. This transfer was never put into effect. The Armenians reopened the question in 1988, which led to an attack by Azeris on the Armenian minority in Sumgait, an industrial city north of Baku. Further attacks followed by each side, leading to a massive movement of refugees. In 1991, Armenia and Azerbaijan agreed to a ceasefire and negotiations, but a solution to the problem has yet to be found, and fighting continues.

An Azeri soldier on the alert

After Stalin's death in 1953, the Soviet Union was led by a series of Communist party members. The wholesale terror of Stalin's time was never successfully reimposed, but the intrinsic inability of the totalitarian system to correct itself eventually led to corruption and decay, culminating in total economic and political collapse.

Prisoners at a Siberian work camp

Joseph Stalin

Marchers mourn those who died in the bloody rally in Tbilisi in April 1989.

GORBACHEV AND GLASNOST

In 1985, when Mikhail Gorbachev became leader of the Soviet Union, the country was in bad shape. The economy was weak, because huge sums had been spent on the military and not enough on modernization and economic expansion. The administration was badly organized and corrupt. Worst of all, the standard of living of most of the people of the Soviet Union was unbelievably low. Many people could not even get enough food and clothes, let alone luxuries.

Perestroika

Gorbachev was the first Soviet leader to tackle these problems. When he came to power, he announced new reform policies of *perestroika*, or rebuilding, and *glasnost*, or openness. He said that everyone could speak freely about their problems and how they wanted things to be run, and he created the Congress of People's Deputies as a forum for such discussion. From the start, Gorbachev said that *perestroika* was a long-term goal and that in the short term things were likely to get worse, rather than better.

Nationalist demonstrations

The countries on the western borders of the Soviet Union, members of the Warsaw Pact, were all beginning to go their own way. For once, the Soviet Union did not crack down to bring these states back into line. For the first time in 70 years, the people of the Soviet Union were able to speak out. *Glasnost* led to the spread of dissatisfaction. Before long, encouraged by events in other Eastern Bloc countries, the murmurings of long-repressed nationalism were heard. At first, Gorbachev did not know how to react, and in some cases the army was sent in. Soviet special troops killed 20 civilian demonstrators in Tbilisi in April 1989, precipitating decisive moves toward independence. Finally, in the face of demonstrations throughout the Soviet Union, Gorbachev allowed people to look into self-government.

Attempted coup

Not everyone in the Soviet Union was happy about Gorbachev's reforms. In August 1991, communist hardliners closely associated with Gorbachev staged an unsuccessful coup, attempting to return the country to totalitarian government by force. The leaders of the coup wanted to bring back many of the worst aspects of Soviet life, including censorship of the press and the powers of the secret police. Gorbachev was placed under arrest in his holiday villa on the Black Sea. The leaders of the coup believed they could return the country to totalitarian rule in the old way by force of military might. But the Soviet

The government house in Yerevan

people proved otherwise! They took to the streets to defend their freedom and within days the coup was overthrown.

End of the Soviet Union

In December 1991, the Soviet Union was officially dissolved. Mikhail Gorbachev, by now the leader of a country that no longer existed, resigned in 1991. Boris Yeltsin, the first genuinely democratically elected leader, became president of the Russian Federation.

Gorbachev meets the Soviet people.

STANDING ALONE

Georgia, Armenia, and Azerbaijan have been independent states since the end of December 1991. As part of the Soviet Union, Transcaucasia relied on the economic and military support of the empire. Now, their independence depends on outside assistance.

Economic problems

In common with the whole of the former Soviet Union, a major issue is the economy. The problems Gorbachev started to address have yet to be solved, and massive sums of foreign investment are needed. The International Monetary Fund (I.M.F.) will help, but in return it expects the new states to opt for a capitalist economy, which they may not necessarily be prepared to do.

The C.I.S. seems set to become an economic union, perhaps on the lines of the European Community (E.C.), and Armenia and Azerbaijan have both now joined. On October 17, 1991, Armenia signed a 3-year agreement with Moscow and seven other former Soviet republics that established a free-trade zone and set up inter-republican bodies controlling finance and banking, food, energy, and industrial supplies.

Turkey's influence

The Nagorno-Karabakh question involves future relations with Turkey. Turkey's President Turgut Ozal warned in March 1992 that he was ready to block landlocked Armenia's only export route to the Black Sea to force Armenians to

Muslims at prayer in Iran

abandon their fight with Azerbaijan for Nagorno-Karabakh. NATO and the C.I.S. have tried to mediate in the dispute, as has Iran.

Turkey is looking for alternatives to its long-delayed acceptance as a member of the E.C., such as a Black Sea cooperation zone. To achieve this, Turkey needs to consolidate relations with Christian Armenia and Georgia. Although Turkey is a firmly secular state, its neighbors recall centuries of Ottoman rule and are wary of Turkey's intentions. Syria and Iraq suspect that Turkey wishes to harness the Tigris and Euphrates rivers.

Iran's role

Turkey's land link to Azerbaijan and the other Islamic republics passes through the Caucasus, and most conveniently through Armenia. Iran sees Armenia as the chess piece blocking Turkey's ambitions. Iran is also concerned about potential conflict with Azerbaijan over the nine million Azeris who live inside its northern border in the Iranian province also called Azerbaijan.

Turgat Ozal, Turkey's president

The positions of Georgia, Armenia, and Azerbaijan among their neighbors are as yet unclear. The intertwined and sometimes competing interests of the three major powers in the region will continue to lead to various alliances and coalitions.

The armed forces of the former Soviet Union are a subject of dispute among the states.

OUTLOOK

At home in all three of the states, the establishment of a democratic government structure is on the agenda. Many political parties have developed since independence, including, in Georgia, two monarchist groups. The heir to the throne of Georgia, which has been unoccupied for nearly two hundred years, is Prince Jorge Bagration, a Spanish-born race-car driver currently living in Marbella, Spain.

The question of minorities

Major issues facing the whole region include the question of minorities such as the Ossetians on the border between Georgia and Russia. The position of Nagorno-Karabakh continues to be a problem, not just in the disputed region itself, but in surrounding areas that are packed with refugees. Between 200,000 and 250,000 refugees are thought to have fled from the Nagorno-Karabakh region.

Tea-growing is a major industry in the area.

Environmental issues

Environmental concerns have come to the fore, too. As throughout the rest of the Soviet Union, industrial pollution is a big problem in the area. Nuclear power stations, such as that at Nayirit in Armenia, are the subject of much disquiet because of fears that they are situated too near the earthquake zone.

Industrial pollution in Transcaucasia is a cause for concern.

Farming in the area depends heavily on irrigation. In Armenia, the productivity of half the farmland depends totally on irrigation. One major concern is the lowering of the water level in Armenia's Lake Sevan, due to demand. There is also soil erosion due to the intensive cultivation of the sloping hillsides.

Development

While foreign aid may help with immediate problems, it is important that Armenia, Georgia, and Azerbaijan develop their own economies as soon as possible. Fortunately, these areas already have certain thriving industries and the potential for further development. Foreign investors have already stepped in to help development in some areas, such as international air links and satellite telephones.

Tourism

Tourism is poised to become a major foreign currency earner when the political

State emblem of Azerbaijan

State emblem of Armenia

situation permits. Black Sea resorts such as Pitsunda have been famous since Tsarist times and were developed for the mass market during the Soviet period. A ski resort opened with Austrian participation at Gudauri in 1987.

Ports

The Georgian Black Sea ports have long been the export and import points for much of the trade from the former Soviet Union. Northern ports such as Murmansk are closed for five months of the year due to ice, making the Black Sea a vital route for shipping. The Georgian port of Batumi is a former Soviet submarine base. Ownership of the U.S.S.R.'s navy was the subject of fierce dispute between Russia and the Ukraine.

Oil

The Azeri oil industry is one of the oldest in the world. In 1900, the Baku oil fields were the most important oil source in the world, producing half the world's supply. Output peaked in 1940. Oil and gas are exported by sea and via a pipeline to Batumi and Yerevan. Azerbaijan's future may depend on its oil.

The future

At the moment, Georgia, Armenia, and Azerbaijan depend on the support of countries around them: Turkey, Iran, and the C.I.S., and on international bodies such as NATO and the I.M.F. They need to develop their own strong economic and political structures very quickly in order to fend off pressure from the rest of the world.

FACTS AND FIGURES

GEORGIA

Area: 26,900 square miles (69,570 square kilometers)
Capital: Tbilisi
Population: 5,500,000 (est. 1989)
Highest mountain: Mkinvari (Kazbek) 16,512 feet (5,033 meters)
Major rivers: Inguri, Rioni, Kodori
Climate: In the west, high rainfall, subtropical temperatures. In the east, drier
Vegetation: Swamp grasses and reeds in the west, oak and beech forests on lower mountain slopes, and fir trees above
Wildlife: Dolphins in the Black Sea, wolves and bears in the forests
Agriculture: Tea, citrus fruits, wine grapes, tobacco
Industry: Minerals, including manganese, coal, and gold. Rich lumber resources. Hydroelectric power
Ethnic mix: 65% Georgian, 10% Armenian, also Russian and Azeris
Language: Georgian, which uses its own alphabet
Religion: Orthodox Eastern Christianity

ARMENIA

Area: 11,306 square miles (29,280 square kilometers)
Capital: Yerevan
Population: 3,500,000 (est. 1991)
Highest mountain: Mount Aragats 13,418 feet (4,090 meters)
Major rivers: Aras
Climate: From dry, hot subtropical to year-round snow on mountains
Vegetation: Semidesert to forest
Wildlife: Wild boar, jackal, wildcat
Agriculture: Livestock, grapes
Industry: Food-processing, machine-building, and chemicals
Ethnic mix: 90 % Armenian, also Azeris, Kurds, Ukrainians, and Russians
Language: Armenian
Religion: Orthodox Eastern Christianity

AZERBAIJAN

Area: 33,400 square miles (86,505 square kilometers)
Capital: Baku
Population: 7,145,000 (est. 1990)
Highest mountain: Bazardyuzyu 14,515 feet (4,424 meters)
Major rivers: Kura, Aras
Climate: Hot, dry summers and cold, wet winters
Vegetation: Forest, steppe, semidesert
Wildlife: Wolves, gazelle, pelican, wildcat
Agriculture: Cotton, tobacco, fruit
Industry: Oil and gas, chemicals. Food-processing
Ethnic mix: 90% Azeri, 10% Russian, except Nagorno-Karabakh, where 80% Armenian
Language: Azeri
Religion: Muslim

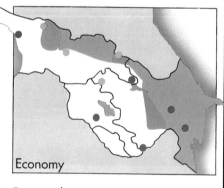

Economy

- Silver
- Gold
- Major power stations
- Oil fields
- Natural gas fields

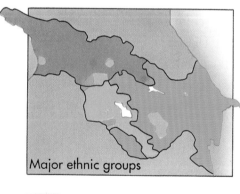

Major ethnic groups

- Georgians
- Armenians
- Azeris

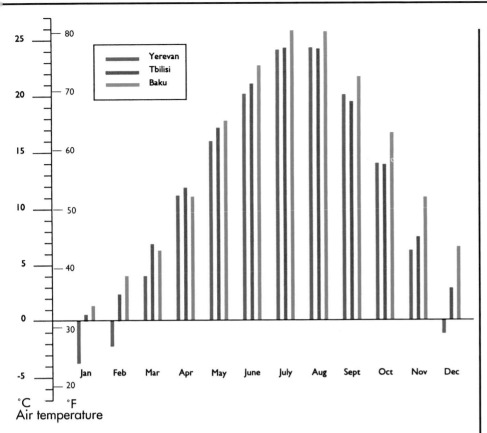

25 — 80
20 — 70
15 — 60
10 — 50
5 — 40
0 — 30
-5 — 20

°C — °F
Air temperature

Yerevan
Tbilisi
Baku

Jan Feb Mar Apr May June July Aug Sept Oct Nov Dec

Climate

The Caucasus Mountains protect Transcaucasia from the extremes of Russia's cold climate. Georgia's climate is mild, dominated by warm air from the Black Sea. Armenia is landlocked, and ninety percent of the land is over 3,300 feet (1,000 meters) high. It is much drier, with hot summers and long, warm autumns. Azerbaijan has more variation in its climate, humid in some areas and dry in others. Although mostly mild, some mountainous areas can be inaccessible for three or four months of the year due to snow.

Industry

Armenia experienced rapid industrial expansion after the revolution, and today has a highly diversified industrial base, including mineral extraction and machine-building. Other states of the Soviet Union took longer to develop. Georgia also depends on mineral extraction and machine-building. For many years, Azerbaijan's industry depended on oil production, but today industries as diverse as engineering and food processing thrive in the country. Baku, one of the former Soviet Union's most beautiful cities, is surrounded by oil derricks.

Agriculture

In spite of the difficulty of working the mountainous land, the three states each have a significant agricultural output. They grow mainly expensive crops such as tea and fruit, maximizing the potential of the small amount of arable land available.

Transportation

Mountains are an impediment to the construction of land routes throughout Transcaucasia. Most rivers are not navigable. In mountainous Armenia, most freight is carried by road. Azerbaijan and Georgia depend more on their rail networks, but many places in these countries too can only be reached by road.

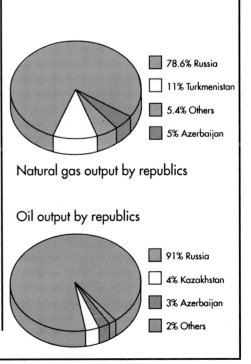

78.6% Russia
11% Turkmenistan
5.4% Others
5% Azerbaijan

Natural gas output by republics

Oil output by republics

91% Russia
4% Kazakhstan
3% Azerbaijan
2% Others

CHRONOLOGY AND FAMOUS PEOPLE

c. 100,000 B.C. First human settlements
7th century B.C. King Mita (Midas)
66 B.C. Pompey invades Caucasus
A.D. 284-361 King Mirian III reigns over eastern Georgia
330 Georgia Christianized
645 Arabs conquer Tbilisi and install emir
885 Ashot, Bagratid prince, becomes king of Armenia
1027-1072 Georgia united under Bagrat IV
1064 Seljuk Turks take Armenian capital Ani
1080 Armenian kingdom of Cilicia founded
1089-1124 King David the Builder: the Golden Age of Georgia
1184-1212 Queen Tamara
1220 Mongol invasion
1334 Mongols driven out
1366 Black Death decimates Georgian population
1386 Tamerlane destroys Tbilisi
1453 Ottoman Turks capture Constantinople
1548 Safavid Turks capture Tbilisi
1801 Georgia

Tsar Peter I (1672-1725) was known as Peter the Great. He traveled widely in Europe and determined to modernize Russia in line with the rest of the continent. He edited Russia's first newspaper and opened the first museum.

incorporated in Russian Empire
1905 First Russian revolution
1914-17 World War I
1917 Bolshevik coup in Petrograd
1917-20 Transcaucasian republics independent
1920 Red Army marches into Baku
1921 Red Army invades Georgia
1922-36 All three countries ruled as a single Transcaucasian republic from Moscow
1936 Armenia becomes

Joseph Stalin was Transcaucasia's most famous son. He was born Joseph Vissarionovich Djugashvili, in Georgia in 1879. As a result of his policies as leader of the Soviet Union, it is estimated that twenty million people died.

Armenian Soviet Socialist Republic; Georgia becomes Georgian S.S.R.; Azerbaijan becomes Azerbaijani S.S.R. within the newly created Soviet Union
1939-45 World War II
1985 Gorbachev announces *perestroika* and *glasnost* in Moscow
December 7, 1988 Armenian earthquake
April 1989 Riots and massacre in Tbilisi
1990 Republics hold first multi-party elections
April 9, 1991 Georgia

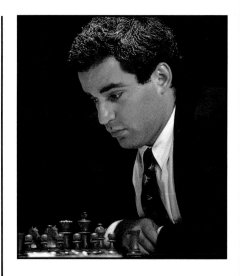

Levon Ter-Petrosyan became the first president of Armenia after independence. Armenia's first foreign minister after independence was Raffi Hovannisian, an Armenian born in California.

Zviad Gamsakhurdiya was Georgia's first president after independence. He was overthrown after five months. Unrest between Gamsakhurdiya's supporters and the present government continues.

Gary Kasparov, born in Baku, is a world famous chess Grand Master. Other famous Transcaucasians of today include Armenian astrophysicist Victor Hainbakaiman and Georgian film director Tengis Abuladze.

declares independence
August 1991 Coup in Moscow fails, but brings down Gorbachev
August 30, 1991 Azerbaijan declares independence

September 1991 Armenia declares independence
December 1991 Gorbachev resigns. Yeltsin declares the Soviet Union dissolved; creation of

Commonwealth of Independent States
1992 Independence for all three republics, Armenia and Azerbaijan join the Commonwealth of Independent States

Mstilav Rostopovish, cellist and composer, was born in Baku in 1927. He has toured many countries, achieving world fame. Armenian composer Aram Khachaturian also enjoys worldwide renown.

INDEX

PHOTOCREDITS